SPELLING RULES OK!

STUART SILLARS

JONQUIL PUBLISHING

CONTENTS

Ⓒ Stuart Sillars 1984

0 946685 01 0

First published 1984

Reprinted 1986

For Laurence, Stephie, Alex and Tim

Illustration concepts by Stuart Sillars

Design by Michael Lopategui

Typeset by Centrepoint Typesetters Ltd

Printed by The Modern Printers

**Jonquil Publishing, Unit 1, Parson's Green Estate,
Boulton Road, Stevenage, Herts.**

Is AND Es 1

'I before e except after c — but only when the sound is ee'.

Sounds silly, really, doesn't it? But it's a good way to remember some of those awkward spellings which nobody's too sure of.

When the sound of a word is ee — as in grief, for example — the i comes before the e. But if there's a c in front, the e comes first — as in ceiling.

So, it's **believe** but deceive, reprieve but **receive.**

Some words like this are very important. If you're thinking of working in a shop or office, **receipt** is sure to crop up a lot. If you want to be a farmer, you'll need to be able to spell **field.**

Make a list of ten words which follow the rule given in the rhyme, and then check them in a dictionary.

Now try these!

1. 'How can I bel____ve he's not dec____ving me?' she wondered.
2. It was a great rel____f to rec____ve your letter.
3. From the window I perc____ved the view across the f____lds to the sea.
4. The th____f was given a repr____ve, which put an end to his gr____f.

He woke to find the c____ling spinning. Then he remembered. He'd rec____ved a message asking him to meet a repr____ved killer in a f____ld outside the city. He'd bel____ved it — dumb sap. It wasn't anything to get conc____ted over, and there was no point in gr____ving. He moved, and it felt as if a bomb went off in his head. Trying to retr____ve the p____ces, he perc____ved a figure knocking on the glass door. That was all he needed!

Is AND Es 2

Some words don't follow the 'i before e except after c' rule. There are **weir, seize** and **science,** for example. Remember them by remembering the pictures. Can you think of another five words which break the rule?

The other part of the rhyme is quite helpful too — 'but only when the sound is ee'.

If the sound isn't ee, then the rule doesn't apply, and the spelling is usually ei. So it's **weight, height** and their. See if you can find some more examples of this part of the rule — use a dictionary to check your ideas.

Now try these!

1. Suddenly he s____zed the r____ns and drove off.
2. His counterf____t coins were the h____ght of perfection.
3. The anc____nt building made the sc____ntist feel w____rd.
4. The w____ght of the evidence was against the th____f.

Sh____la was worr____d. It was w____rd. She bel____ved that K____th was dec____ving her, and she v____wed th____r br____f romance with gr____f. Was his love counterf____t? ____ther it was, or the n____ghbours were lying. Suddenly she felt quite anc____nt. How could she retr____ve his love, s____ze his affection, and really ach____ve something?

PLURALS WITH S

It's usually quite easy to make plurals — words for more than one of something. You just add an s to the word for one of whatever it is. So it's cats, bulldozers, cassettes, tracks.

Almost all words can be turned into plurals by adding s, but not quite all — and that's where the problems start.

Words ending in ch are made plural by adding **es.** This is quite a sensible rule when you think about it: words like this would be very hard to say without the extra sound! Ditch becomes ditches, witch — witches, bench — **benches,** pitch — pitches, sandwich — sandwiches.

Words ending in o aren't so easy. Some have plurals ending in es, but others just add an s for the plural. It's potatoes and dominoes, but just plain tomatoes, discos and **videos.** There isn't a rule about which add s and which add es, so you need to be extra careful about words like these.

Try thinking of some more words ending in ch or o and working out their plurals. Then check them in a dictionary.

Words ending in y form their plurals in one of two ways. If there's a vowel before the y — a, e, o or u — you just add s. **Monkeys,** donkeys, keys, surveys, guys, plays, trays and boys.

If there isn't a vowel before the y, the plural is formed by taking off the y and adding **ies** in its place. Fly becomes flies, cry changes into cries, gantry to gantries, factory to **factories**. Can you think of any more?

Now try these!

Change the words in brackets into plurals.

In the late nineteen-(eighty), most (family) spent many (hour) a day watching (video). (Domino) lay abandoned, (disco) were empty, (potato) stayed unpeeled. (Meal) were quick (sandwich) snatched between (cassette). (Cry) of grief came from (writer) of (play) and (proprietor) of (theatre) and (gallery). (Factory) crumbled, and (wrench) rusted on garage (workbench). Space (invader) had conquered: (video) ruled the (wave)!

PLURALS WITHOUT S

Although most words can be made into plurals by adding s, or a group of letters ending in s, there are lots which aren't quite so straightforward.

Some foreign words, for example, form their plurals by adding an x at the end. The most common are **bureau** and gateau.

Some words don't change at all in the plural. The plural of deer is deer, and the plural of sheep is **sheep.** Must be confusing for a sheep, stuck on a hillside in Wales all day wondering how many of you there are! Some words for kinds of food don't change either: grapefruit is the most common of them. Another word which doesn't change in the plural is craft; it can mean either one ship or any number of them. The same is true when it's part of a longer word: aircraft and hovercraft can be either singular or plural.

There are some words which change completely in the plural. Goose becomes geese, and mouse becomes **mice.** Spouse — wife or husband — is spouses, not spice, though.

There are some words which don't do what you'd expect. Woman, for example: one is woman, with an a, but two or more are **women,** with an e. Men are just the same: one man, several men.

Now try these!

Change the words in brackets into plurals.

1. A fleet of (hovercraft) delivered (gateau) to the lighthouse.
2. During the winter, food was dropped to the (sheep) by (aircraft).
3. The (man) and (woman) had brought their (spouse) with them.
4. The (goose) were disturbed by the (man) on bicycles.

Noah II: The epic story of two (spacecraft) full of creatures from a doomed planet. They took only (deer), and (horse), and (sheep), and (goose). They chose brilliant (man) and (woman) to crew the (craft). They fed them a special diet of (grapefruit) and low-calorie (gateau). Blasting off from the highest (plateau), the (craft) rocketed into hyperspace.

— ADDING ABLE, IBLE, UBLE —

Forms of words ending in **able** are a useful way of communicating a particular feature of something or someone. If you know about something, for example, you're knowledgeable. If something breaks easily, it's **breakable**. If something is worth laughing about, it's **laughable**.

If the word ends in a consonant — any letter except a, e, i, o u or y, — then with most words you can simply add able to the end to make the new word.

If the word ends in an e, ask yourself if the letter before the e is a c or a g. If it is, does it sound like the c in service or the g in change?

If so, the word keeps its last e, and you just add able as usual. So service becomes serviceable, and change becomes **changeable.**

If the letter before the e isn't a c or g, or if it doesn't sound like the c in service or the g in change, take off the last e before adding able. Love turns into lovable, survive becomes survivable, and argue becomes arguable.

However, it isn't always quite so simple. Some words, like likeable, keep the e even though.they don't have a c or a g.

Then there are words ending in y, like pity and vary. In these, the y changes to an i, to give pitiable and variable.

Then there's **soluble** — that ends in **uble,** and doesn't follow any of the usual rules.

Not all words end in able. Some end in **ible;** for example, there are terrible**,** horrible, credible, **convertible,** deductible and reducible.

Now try these!

Complete these words by adding able, ible or uble. Change or leave out the last letter if you need to.

You know how change_____ he is, like_____ one minute, unmanage_____ the next. Quite pity_____ really — almost laugh_____.

There he was being knowledge_____, and then suddenly he was angry and horr_____. It was a terr_____ sight. It's an insol_____ problem now. He's very love_____ really, but so vary_____; his temper's ungovern_____. It's just unbear_____: like living with the Incred_____ Hulk!

5

ADDING ING

When you add **ing** to a word to show that what you're doing is going on for a while, you often need to change the spelling of the word you're using.

If the word has an e at the end, then it usually loses the e before you add ing.

A few words keep the e, though. Ageing — getting older — is one of the most frequent, and another is queueing.

Another group contains those which end in a double e, like see, foresee and flee. They keep both es, and become **seeing,** foreseeing and fleeing.

There are special rules for words like die and tie, which end in ie. You can't write dieing, or tiing: so in these words, ie changes to y to give **dying** and tying. Dyeing (changing the colour of cloth) is spelt with an e.

Words ending in y are straightforward. They stay the same, and you just add ing after the y. Be careful not to leave out the y — it's **studying,** not studing, which sounds rather nasty. And it's flying, relaying, frying.

STUDYING

Now try these!

Complete the sentences by adding ing to the words in brackets.

1. He was busy (make) sure that somebody was (care) for his aged aunt.
2. I felt sure he was (drive) me mad by constantly (phone) me during the night.
3. (Tie) an apron round his waist he began (fry) the meat.
4. (See) that they were (queue) up, he realised he was in for a (try) time.
5. Although she was (age) rapidly, she kept (study) for her exams.

(See) the buffalo (graze), he realised something was wrong. They were (raise) their heads, (breathe) quickly. Now they were (move) — no, (stampede), (flee) from the fire that was (pursue) them. Next moment he was (phone) headquarters, (relay) news of the fire to the city, (try) to get them to evacuate. No use (argue): it was (spread) fast. The bush was (blaze) — and it didn't smell at all like (fry) steak!

ADDING LY

It's often useful to be able to say how something was done. Words that do this are called adverbs, and many of them can be formed by adding **ly** to the end of other words.

Words ending in l also follow a simple rule. Just add another l and a y. Occasional becomes occasionally, usual becomes usually, thoughtful and careful change to **thoughtfully** and carefully.

Then there are those words which end in ic. These usually take ally when they change into adverbs. Scientific changes to **scientifically,** and automatic to automatically.

Be careful, though; public changes to publicly, and doesn't follow the rule at all.

There's a simple rule for words which end in y. Take off the y and add ily. So busy becomes busily, happy changes to happily, angry to angrily.

The last group are those words which end in e. If the letter before the e is a or u, simply knock off the e and add ly. True changes to **truly** and due to duly, for example.

All others ending in e just take ly as usual — brave becomes bravely, free — freely, large — largely.

Now try these!

Add ly to the words in brackets to complete the sentences.

1. 'I speak French, Spanish and Italian (fluent),' she snapped (angry).
2. (Happy), the house was not damaged too (bad) by the fire.
3. (Usual) he wrote most (careful), but now he scribbled (erratic).
4. She was (true) angry that he had announced it (public).
5. (Scientific) speaking, evidence of ghosts is (large) unreliable.

The castle was (glorious) sited on a cliff which looked (menacing) down on a (tortuous) rocky shore. It was (cunning) located: anyone trying to break in would have to do it very (wary). He tried to climb (scientific) but (real) felt rather scared. Inching (brave) along, he (careful) rested his foot on a ledge. It fell away (immediate), and he was left hanging (sickening) above a (fearful) deep drop.

7

── MAKING OPPOSITES 1 ──

Negatives are opposites — that is, versions of words which mean the opposite of what the word first meant.

Some words can't be turned into negatives: nobody says that something is 'ungood', for example.

Many words, though, can be turned into negatives just by adding a few letters at the front.

The most usual letters to add are **un.** Helpful becomes unhelpful, kind becomes unkind. Others include unbearable, unable, unfamiliar, and those shown in the drawings. Find some more yourself in a dictionary.

Another group of negatives starts with **im;** impatient, improbably and immoral.

Then there are those which start with **in;** indestructible, inadequate, informal.

You can find lots more ins and ims in the dictionary, but be careful: not all of them are negatives of other words. Intense and impact, for example, are complete words on their own.

Another group begins with **ir.** There aren't as many of these words, and they're mainly formed from words which begin with r. Irresponsible and irrational are good examples — and so is irreplaceable.

Now try these!

1. It was highly ____likely that such an ____formal man was not ____tidy in his habits.
2. Their attitude to the ____firm was ____kind and ____helpful.
3. He was very ____patient with the ____responsible and ____practical young man.
4. It was ____probable that the ____replaceable paintings had survived the fire.

Well darling, I knew it was ____responsible, but I didn't think it was ____moral. Poor ____sophisticated me! I was quite ____prepared for it, and thought it awfully ____proper. He said it would be very ____formal, but I felt so ____adequate and ____prepared. He said it was ____likely we'd be seen and he was so ____patient. It was all so ____familiar. But, do you know it wasn't at all ____pleasant. I quite enjoyed eating jellied eels with chopsticks!

——MAKING OPPOSITES 2——

Many words can be turned into negatives, with the opposite of their first meaning, by adding **dis** at the beginning.

Dislike is one of the most common, and others include disagree and disloyal.

Others form their negative by adding **il** at the front. Usually these are words which begin with l. There are illogical and illegible — and, of course, **illegal.**

There are some negatives which aren't quite so straightforward. Some words, for example, are turned into negatives by adding **ill-,** with a hyphen, at the beginning. **Ill-natured,** ill-mannered and ill-tempered are useful ones to know.

Some words have to make do with having non- stuck on at the front. **Non-hazardous** is a good one, and so is non-inflammable, meaning something which will not burn.

Then there's **abnormal,** the only useful negative form which starts with **ab** — check in the dictionary if you don't believe me. And, while you're looking at a dictionary, try finding some more negatives starting with dis and il.

Now try these!

1. He was very _____agreeable, and argued in an ____logical way.
2. The writing was quite ____legible, and the whole thing looked _____honest and ____legal.
3. The ____normal load contained _____hazardous chemicals.
4. She was _____natured and _____tempered.

And another thing, Roger — you're the most _____courteous, _____mannered and _____agreeable man I've met. I'm sure you're up to all sorts of ____legal activities even though you say they're ____hazardous. If you're not openly _____honest then everything you do is ____normal and ____logical. I don't want to seem_____loyal, Roger, but you're just an _____bred lout.

APOSTROPHES 1

Apostrophes are those strange things looking like commas, which float about near the ends of some words and in the middle of others.

They show that a letter, or small group of letters, has been left out of a word.

Think of a simple one — I am. Say it a few times quickly, and you'll see that the a gets lost, and the word turns into **I'm.**

He is changes into **he's,** we are to we're, they are to they're, it is to **it's.** To make the meaning clear, the apostrophe goes above the space where the letters have been left out.

As well as these simple expressions, you can use an apostrophe for more complicated ones. I've is the shorter form of I have, he's of he has, and we've, you've and they've are easier versions of we have, you have and they have.

The same is true of lots of other words. I will, you will and they will change to I'll, you'll and they'll.

Had, should and would often shorten to 'd, as in **I'd,** You'd, **he'd,** we'd. Could have changes to could've, should have to should've, and would have to would've.

Now try these!

Shorten the words in brackets by using apostrophes.

1. (They are) sure that (they have) everything (we are) going to need.
2. He says (he has) studied electronics, but (I am) not sure I believe him.
3. I (would have) done it myself if I (could have) been there in time.
4. (You will) see: (they will) be here in the morning.
5. (He had) forgotten everything he (should have) remembered.

Look squire, if (I had) taken the jewels I (should have) sold them by now. So will he: he (would have) taken them to a fence — or he (should have) done — to get rid of 'em, see! (It is) no use grilling me. (He would) never have told me where (he is) thinking of going. (I would) get on to Amsterdam, if I were you — (that is) where I (would have) gone, (I am) sure. He (could have) gone to Paris, but (they are) bad payers there. Bet you a fiver (he has) sold them in Amsterdam: (it is) what I (would have) done, straight up, guv!

APOSTROPHES 2

Apostrophes in words like I'm and could've show that a letter or two have been left out to make the word easier to say. The same is true when you use an apostrophe in words which describe things which do not happen.

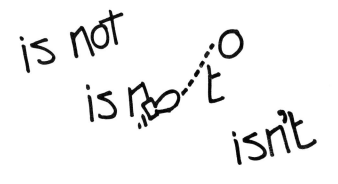

Think about is not, for example. Most people would say **isn't** instead. Again, the apostrophe goes where the letter has been left out. Notice that the two words have joined into one — isn't — and that there's no break, and no apostrophe, between them.

So, do not becomes don't: does not becomes doesn't: did not becomes didn't. The same is true of haven't, couldn't, shouldn't, wouldn't, wasn't and weren't.

There's also another group of words which is a little more complicated. The two words have been combined again, and the apostrophe goes over the space where the letters have been left out: but the words have changed slightly too. For example, will not becomes won't, and shall not becomes **shan't.** The leaving-out has gone a step further, making the words a lot easier to say.

One more completes the set — can't. This is a shortened form of cannot.

Now try these!

Shorten the words in brackets by using apostrophes.

1. I (would not) be too happy if I were you: we (have not) finished yet.
2. You (should not) talk like that, even if you (do not) mean it.
3. He (cannot) understand that they (will not) be visiting him.
4. (Cannot) they come tomorrow? I (shall not) be in on Tuesday.

Right, you miserable crew. I (would not) give you houseroom if I (was not) getting paid for it. (Do not) come the sob stories — I (would not) like to break your little hearts, not that I (could not). It (is not) fair, is it sonny? You (should not) have joined, should you? I (have not) got time to waste, so I (will not) keep telling you: you (cannot) get away with it and you (will not) get away with it. The Brigadier (does not) like sloppy soldiers, so we (do not) give him sloppy soldiers, do we, sonny? Is that clear or (is not) it?

APOSTROPHES 3

All apostrophes are there to show that a letter or group of letters have been left out — even those you use to show something belongs to someone.

A long time ago, instead of saying the book's cover, the sheep's tail, or the boy's shirt, you'd have said the bookes cover, the sheepes tail and the boyes shirt.

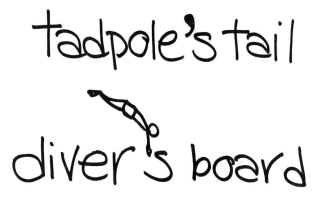

There didn't seem a lot of point in having that extra e, so a lot of go-ahead, trendy people in the sixteenth century started leaving it out — and an apostrophe took its place.

So today, when you need to show that something belongs to someone, or that it's part of something else, all you need do is add an apostrophe and an s at the end — **diver's board, tadpole's tail, George's dog.**

Words for more than one of something — plurals — don't have apostrophes, and neither do any other words which just end in s, like glass, success, possess, for example. Unless you're writing about something belonging to, or being part of, something else, don't use an apostrophe.

When you're talking about something belonging to a plural word ending in s, there's a simple rule to follow.

Put an apostrophe at the end of the word, but don't add another s. So it's the **dogs' collars,** not the dogs's collars — the ziz sound on the end would be very clumsy, so the s isn't added.

If the plural word doesn't end in an s, though, add an apostrophe and an s as usual. Examples of this are the children's books, fishermen's nets, servicemen's pay, and **women's movement.**

Now try these!

Add apostrophes where they're needed in this passage.

The doctors patients sat looking at papers in the waiting-rooms gloom. The old ladys daughter read her womens magazine, and the parsons wife looked at a friends knitting patterns. The receptionists in-tray was piled with letters and files and patients records. Along the corridor, cries came from the childrens clinic. 'Next!' shouted the receptionists assistant.

HEAR, HERE; WEAR, WHERE

Two words which sound the same but have quite different meanings are hear and here.

Hear is what you do with your ears. A good way of remembering how to spell it is by thinking of ear with an h in front.

The second one — **here** — is more to do with eyes than ears. It's a place near enough to see. Think of it as it's shown in the drawing.

Here is also the one you use in expressions like 'look here' or 'here it is'.

Now try these!

1. Stand h_____ and see if you can _____ anything unusual.
2. 'Look h_____,' he said, 'you must be h_____ing things: there's no one h_____.'
3. 'I h_____ you've had some trouble down h_____,' he said.
4. She said 'H_____ we are again then,' but nobody could h_____ her.

Another pair which sometimes causes problems is wear and where.

Wear has two meanings. First, it's what you do with clothes. Secondly, it's what happens to things with age — they wear away.

The other **where** is to do with finding your way, as in 'where are you?'. You could think of it as here with a w in front of it, or you could remember it as it's shown in the drawing.

Now try these!

5. It was the kind of place w_____ you could w_____ whatever you liked.
6. He looked down to w_____ the river had begun to w_____ away the supports of the bridge.
7. The coat had started to w_____ badly w_____ the sleeves joined the yoke.

   H_____, on this tropical paradise, w_____ the only sound is the waves w_____ing away the sandy beaches, people w_____ what they like and go w_____ they please. You can h_____ little except the waves, for, on an island w_____ everyone has everything, w_____'s the sense in talking? The silence is w_____ing only for those who miss the world of business, w_____ life is governed by profits which are h_____ today and now_____ tomorrow. But you won't h_____ many complaints h_____, w_____ even buying h_____ing-aid batteries is too much like hard work!

ITS, IT'S

A book belonging to Peter is Peter's book, right? Right.

A cassette belonging to Sharon is Sharon's cassette, right? Right.

A bowl belonging to a stray dog is it's bowl, right? Wrong.

That's the problem with it in a nutshell.

Usually, when something belongs to somebody or something else, you add an apostrophe and an s. There are exceptions, though, and the most important are these:

His = something belonging to him
Hers = something belonging to her
Its = something belonging to it

Not one of them has an apostrophe. They are very often mis-spelt, mainly because people put in apostrophes which shouldn't be there.

Now try these!

1. She was sure that the things were
_____, but he kept saying they were
_____.

2. The dog sat on her lap, _____ face close
to _____.

3. Suddenly _____ self-control broke, and his outburst was frightening in _____ violence.
4. _____ arguments were put forcefully, but _____ were more sensible.

There are times, though, when you need to write it's with an apostrophe. Then, the word has a completely different meaning:

It's = It is

Over the years, people have combined the two words it and is. It's is much easier to say than it is.

When you're not sure which one to use — its or it's — ask yourself if the meaning is 'something belonging to it' or 'it is'. The one that refers to the dog's bowl is its. The one to use in phrases like 'it's cold' or 'it's Tuesday' is it's.

Now try these!

I_____ just not right, chief. I_____ not starting properly, and the slow running is on the blink. Perhaps i_____ the big end that's gone — i____ noisy too, you see. I_____ petrol consumption's up — and i_____ a thirsty car anyway. I_____ strange: I hope

i_____ something small that's wrong. I_____ choke needs careful handling — i_____ easy to stall it. Still, i_____ up to you now, chief — I'm sure you'll sort out i_____ little problems.

KNOT, NOT; NO, KNOW, NOW

Knot and not are a troublesome pair, with the same sound but quite different meanings.

Knot is the one that you tie in string or rope. Try thinking of the drawing to remember that first k.

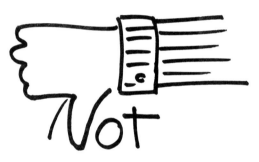

Not is the one about negative things: not open, not available, or not present. Think of it as it's shown in the drawing — a thumbs down sign.

No is clear enough — it's the opposite of yes, and the word which stops or prohibits in notices or statements, such as 'no entry' or 'no parking'.

Know is rather different — it means to 'be certain' or 'sure of something. Think of it as something rock hard, an absolute certainty.

These two are made a little more confusing by the word **now**. The meaning is clear enough, but it's easy to get muddled up between the three when you're writing. Think of now as a very important occasion — perhaps the vital start of a race.

Now try these!

1. He had been presented with a _____ty problem, by which he was _____ going to be beaten.
2. Although there was _____ a hope of escape, he twisted his body against the _____s that bound it until there was _____ an ounce of energy left in him.
3. I have ____ idea what things are like _____, but I _____ how they were.
4. '_____, we can't decide _____. I _____ it sounds weak, but we must delay our decision a little longer.'

I _____ its _____ been easy for you, and you've had _____ty problems to solve, but I also _____ it's _____ hardship to you, and that _____ you _____ what it's all about, there'll be ____ more uncertainty. We've _____ much time _____, so there's ____ point in worrying. Tie yourselves in with slip _____s, and there's to be ____ talking _____ that we've set off. And remember: there's ____ turning back _____. Once you've jumped out of the plane, you're on your own!

15

THERE, THEIR, THEY'RE

These three words all sound the same but mean quite different things.

There is the most common; it has three separate meanings.

It means there as in 'over there' — a place somewhere in the distance which is the opposite of here.

It can also be used in the expression 'there is' or 'there are'. This meaning is rather like the first one, except that, instead of pointing to a place, it can point to an idea, or anything that's been noticed.

The word there is also used as an exclamation. When somebody falls over a carpet you've told him to nail down for the past six weeks, you might well say 'There! I told you so!' You can also use this word to comfort someone, as in 'there there'.

Their has quite a different meaning — something belonging to them: their books and their time. Whenever you're describing something belonging to them, there is the one you want.

They're is something else again. It's a shortened version of 'they are', with an apostrophe standing for the a that's been left out. Think of it as part of a longer phrase, like 'they're after us' or 'they're taking over'.

Now try these!

1. 'Th_____ down th_____,' she said nervously.
2. Th_____ was no reason why the children should not have taken th_____ pets to school today.
3. 'Th_____ all mad over th_____: th_____ is no sense in what they say.'
4. Th_____ clothes were torn, but th_____ was an air of importance about them.

'Th_____!' she said. 'I know they are th_____!'
'Nonsense,' I replied. 'Th_____'s no one th_____!'

'Th_____ getting closer, I tell you,' she insisted. 'I can hear th_____ voices, and smell th_____ breath. Oh Charles, th_____ terrible!'
'Th_____'s no need to get excited,' I replied. 'Th_____ may be someone th_____, but if th_____ is, then th_____ certainly not coming any closer.' By now I, too, felt that th_____ were some strange beings out th_____. 'If th_____ th_____, I'll find them!' I said. I stepped out — and felt a blow on the back of my head. 'Th_____! she said. 'I told you! They're there!'

TO, TOO, TWO

These three words can seem quite confusing, but taken one at a time their meanings are a lot clearer.

To is the most common. Often it's used to indicate a direction — to the shops, to India, even being sent to Coventry. It's a signpost, saying where somebody or something is going to.

You can also use to as a signpost for what you're going to do next. If you want to stay or to go, to watch a video or to read a book, it's the same word you need to use.

So, to spelt with one o is a signpost for both directions and actions.

Too has a different meaning: it can mean 'as well', as in 'this, too, is important'. It's a link to join things together, and is quite different from the other to.

Then there's the second meaning of too: too much of something. You use this one in expressions like 'too hot', 'too cold', 'too dark', or 'too expensive'. Or, in the case of the famous spoiled broth, 'too many'.

The last one is the number **two** — the awkward one with w in the middle. You'll need it particularly for writing a sum of money in figures, on a cheque or a giro.

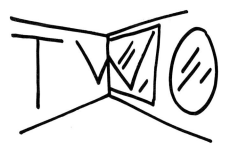

Now try these!

1. As there were t____ sets of twins, it was t____ complicated t____ tell them apart.
2. It was t____ much of a coincidence that t____ people had come t__ ask me about the accident on the same day.
3. T____ swans circled the pond lazily, and then came down t____ land a little t__ _ far away from me.
4. He was t____ dazed t__ be certain, but he thought there were t____ people in the lane t__ his right.

When I got t__ the gates, it was t____ foggy to see very much. Then, t__ the left of the drive, t____ figures crept forward. They came out t____ the lawn, getting closer t__ me all the time. My hand crept t__ my pocket: I was glad t__ feel my revolver. The t____ men came up t__ the gate! They were bound t__ see me soon. T__ stop making any noise, I held my breath. But it was t____ late: they had seen me. Ought I t__ shoot? No; that would be t____ simple . . .

17

WEATHER, WHETHER; THREW, THROUGH

One pair of words with the same sound and different meanings is weather and whether.

Weather is the one we all moan about — rain, sleet, snow and the odd day of sun.

Whether, the other one, is the one you use when not knowing what to do. You don't know whether to go or not, or whether to go with George or with Julie, or whether to watch television or wash your hair. Think of this word as a finely balanced choice between two things, as it is in the drawing.

Another awkward pair is threw and through.

Threw is the past tense of throw, as in 'he threw the ball over the touch line'.

The other one — **through** — is used to describe passing through something, from one side to the other. You could try thinking of it as 'through the looking glass', or as going through a tunnel, as shown in the drawing. It can also mean 'because of' — 'through your action, I've succeeded'.

Now try these!

1. I don't know w_____ the w_____ will change this evening.
2. There's nothing we can do except see w_____ we can w_____ the storm.
3. She reached the summit entirely th_____ her own efforts, looked th_____ her binoculars, and th_____ up her hands in horror.
4. The sudden attack th_____ him off his guard, but somehow he got th_____ it and th_____ his attacker to the ground.

W_____ or not the w_____ held, he had to get th_____. He coiled the rope and th_____ it th_____ the darkness. W_____ he'd been heard or not he couldn't tell, but he had to go th_____ with it. He th_____ a glance behind him and hauled himself along the rope. He made heavy w_____ of it, and in a few minutes had rubbed th_____ his thick gloves. W_____ he succeeded depended on the w_____: he pulled on the rope, and in a moment was th_____ the tunnel and in day-light. He th_____ his gloves behind a rock and walked on, enjoying the bright summer w_____.

18

WHO'S, WHOSE; THEIRS THERE'S,

Two words which often give problems are who's and whose. They sound the same, but mean two different things.

Who's with an apostrophe is short for 'who is'. If you want to ask 'who's coming with me?' or 'who's going to tell him?' this is the one you use.

It can also be short for 'who has', as in 'who's let the cat out?'. It's easier to remember this word by thinking of its full meaning — who is or who has, and this will also tell you when to use who's and when to use whose.

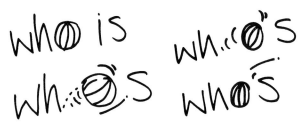

The second word — **whose** — means 'something belonging to whom'. It's 'the woman whose car is outside' or 'whose book is this?'. You use it in all situations like these. Remember that it's one word in its own right, not two combined, like who's — that way you shouldn't get confused between them.

There's and theirs are also confusing.

Theirs means simply 'something which belongs to them,' as in 'the party was theirs'.

Try thinking of whose and theirs together, the first asking a question about ownership, and the second answering it. Whose is it? It's theirs.

There's is short for 'there is' or 'there has' — as, for example, in 'there's a lot of snow outside' or 'there's been an accident'. Like who's, it's much easier to get right if you think of it as two words shortened to one.

there has

there has

there has

there's

Now try these!

'It's all very well to say it's th_____,' I said, 'but th_____ such a thing as responsibility. W_____ going to pay for it? If it's th_____, th_____ no reason why they shouldn't.' 'I don't know w_____ it is,' he said, 'and th_____ no need to take it out on me.' 'If it's th_____,' I said, 'they've got to

move it, and if it isn't, we've got to find out w_____ it is. Th_____ no more to be said,' I said. Well, today it had gone — and we still don't know if it was th_____, or w_____ it was, or w_____ paid to move it. Th_____ something funny going on . . .

YOUR, YOU'RE

It's easy to get muddled about your and you're — but they are really quite different.

The first one shows that something belongs to you, as in '**your** money or your life'.

You're, on the other hand, is a shorter version of 'you are'. Try saying 'you are' quickly a few times, and you'll soon see how the a gradually disappeared: it's much easier to say you're than you are.

Of course, there are more interesting explanations of how the a vanished. Cut out each of these boxes, staple them together at the left and flick them through quickly. The whole story will then flash before you in glorious black and white.

YOU ARE	YOU ARE
YOU ARE	YOU ARE
YOU ARE	YOU'RE
YOU'RE	YOU'RE

Now try these!

Y_____ a rat, Luigi. Y_____ face is gonna get changed, you bet your life. Not that y_____ fit to live, Luigi. When the boss hears of y_____ mistakes y_____ a dead parrot. Be sad if all y_____ windows got broken, wouldn't it? But y_____ not gonna put us to that trouble, are ya? Y_____ not worth the price of a brick, anyway. Don't get y_____ library books renewed, Luigi, 'cos y_____ not gonna get to read them. Y_____ bottle's gone, Luigi, and y_____ gonna join it soon. So mind y_____ step; y_____ friends are watching you. We're fond of ya, Luigi baby — so fond we're gonna put ya out of y_____ misery, soon as we get the chance. Y_____ miserable life's as good as over. Say y_____ prayers, Luigi: y_____ gonna need to, 'cos y_____ a dead man, Luigi.

ACCEPT, EXCEPT

You've probably noticed that there are some particularly nasty words which go about in twos or threes, sounding alike but meaning quite different things. It's worth while trying to sort them out.

A couple which often cause problems are accept and except. The first means 'to take or receive', the second 'apart from'.

You **accept** a present, congratulations and a tricky situation.

You're happy, **except** for one problem. Be careful, too, about the word exception, which means 'odd one out' and is also used in the expression 'take exception' which means 'object'.

It's not quite so easy, though. There's also **expect,** which somehow manages to write itself when you mean to write except. If you expect something, you think it's going to happen, or look forward to it.

Now try these!

1. I didn't _____ your gift, but I _____ it with much pleasure.
2. They were all there _____ Jones, who had not _____ed the invitation.
3. I find it hard to _____ the _____ions to the rule.
4. I _____ you all to be there tomorrow, with no _____ions.
5. He had high _____ations of everybody _____ himself.
6. After a while, she _____ed that she couldn't _____ anything better.

Well, what did you _____? You wanted the job, so you can't _____ to have it all your own way. There are no _____ions. It's the same for all of us. _____ it: you have to go along with things as they are. _____ for you, everybody's happy. I agree with some of your criticisms, but there are some I take _____ion to. I _____ to be blamed for things that go wrong, but there are _____ions which I don't like. If you can't _____ it, you can try being head-teacher yourself, and see how that fulfils your _____ations!

LEAD, LED; BOUGHT, BROUGHT

Lead and led often cause problems.

Lead — pronounced 'leed' — is what you do to a dog, and you do it now, in the present.
Led — pronounced 'ledd' — is what you've done in the past — you may have led your dog home yesterday, or led someone into committing a crime.

Things are made a little more tricky by the word **lead** — pronounced 'ledd' — as in piping, pencils and church roofs.

Today's dog-walk — pronounced 'leed' — is always spelt lead. Led (yesterday's dog-walk) and lead (church roofs) — both pronounced 'ledd'— can be confusing. If you're not sure which you need, ask yourself if you're writing about having walked the dog or about heavy metal. The first is led: the second is lead.

Another awkward pair are bought and brought. Although they sound very similar, they're actually about two quite different things.

Bought means that you've purchased something.

Brought means that you've carried something with you to a particular place.

Now try these!

1. Although he confessed to stealing the l_____ from the roof, he said he'd been l_____ to it by his brother.
2. She began to l_____ the dog away down the road that l_____ to the canal, feeling sad that all her efforts had l_____ to failure.
3. I've b_____ you a present but I haven't b_____ it with me.
4. He b_____ a length of rope and b_____ it back home, together with the groceries he had b_____.

Your honour, I know I've b_____ shame on my family by stealing the l_____. I've l_____ an honest life, but was l_____ astray by an unfortunate accident. I b_____ a bottle of whisky and drank it. When I woke up, someone was l_____ing me to the church. I could've b_____ as much l_____ as I wanted, but by then I was being l_____ up a ladder — I suppose the other bloke had b_____ it with him. Then the police came, and l_____ me down and b_____ me here. Before they l_____ me away, yer honour — d'you want some cheap l_____?

LOOSE, LOSE; CHOOSE, CHOSE;OF, OFF

It's easy to get confused over loose and lose.

Loose is used about teeth, screws and boards.

Lose, on the other hand, is what people do with dogs, tickets, keys and (sometimes) their tempers.

Choose and chose are difficult too, but for a different reason.

Choose is what you do now — select one thing out of several.

Chose has the same meaning, but in the past: I choose one thing today, but chose another yesterday.

Of and off are another awkward couple.

Of is about being part of something, or what it's made from: a box of matches, a heap of coins, a book of stamps, the ace of clubs, and expressions like 'of course' are examples.

Off is more complicated. You go off to work, cut off a piece of wood, or take off a wheel. If you're late for lunch, you'll be told 'chips are off, love!'

It's easy to write of when you mean off, so you need to think carefully when writing it.

Now try these!

1. He ch__se to stay behind and mend the l____se board.
2. To ch____se the wrong one now would be to l____se everything.
3. Suddenly he jumped out o_____ his chair, took his jacket o_____ and dashed o_____ down the corridor.
4. The room was full o_____ smoke. Two men were fighting on a table, and he saw them fall o_____ onto the floor in a whirl o_____ fists.

We c_____ to l_____ no time, and set o_____ straight away. Our route lay through the roughest part o_____ the desert, full o_____ strange perils and quite cut o_____. Should we l_____ our way, no one would find us, and vultures would pick o_____ our flesh until we joined the rest o_____ the l_____ bones in the desert. Not something either of us would c_____. We made sure nothing was l_____ on the truck, to keep flies o_____ our food and out o_____ the petrol cans, and drove o_____. I c_____ to drive first, while Georgina nodded o_____ under some l_____ blankets.

— STATIONARY, STATIONERY;— QUITE, QUIET

Stationary and stationery form a well-known double act which causes a lot of confusion.

One of them — **stationary** — means 'standing still'.

The other — **stationery** — is a word for paper, envelopes, notebooks and that sort of thing.

Quite and quiet aren't easy either. Their meanings are totally (or quite) different.

Quite has two opposite meanings — 'very' or 'completely', as in 'she was quite overcome', and 'partly', as in 'the shops are quite full today'.

Quiet is to do with silence, or with things being not busy.

There aren't many other words made from the four on this page. There's only one that's used at all often — **quietly,** just ly tacked on to quiet.

Now try these!

1. She worked in a small s_____ shop in the centre of the town.
2. He waited until the bus was s_____, and then jumped off.
3. The garden was q_____ still, and birds sang q_____ly in the trees.
4. It was deathly q_____ in the old warehouse: I felt q_____ afraid.

Q_____ please! Right. This is the s_____ van, which will be s_____ outside the office supplies shop next to the bank. Ern, you'll be in the shop looking at s_____. Alf, you'll be standing still outside: well, not q_____ still, not exactly s_____, but moving about q_____ slowly. As soon as the smoke grenades go off, Ern, you run q_____ly out of the s_____ shop, past the s_____ van and into the bank. Do the heist q_____ly; no rough stuff. Come out quickly, into the s_____ van, which will be moving slowly because Bert'll have got it going by then, and we're away. Got it? Not q_____? Then you haven't been listening: I'll tell you again. Q_____ please!

——DIFFICULT WORDS 1——

However many spelling rules you try to work out, some words are awkward.

Take **business,** for instance. The way you spell it and the way you say it seem totally different. You can try thinking of it as busi-ness, the state of being busy, or you could think of it as bus-in-ess. as it's shown in the drawing.

Definite is another odd one. It's the last i that's the problem — it seems so much more sensible to have an a there. But i it is, and it stays there for all the other forms of the word too — definition, definitely and definitive. Think of it as a big, forceful word determined to have its own way.

Separate is a strange one, too. That second vowel is definitely an a, not an e. That's true of other versions of the word too — separately, separation and separated.

It's easy to mis-spell **similar.** The last a is the problem here — it often gets turned into an e. Think of the a in same if you find it hard to remember — similar means the same, too.

Now try these!

1. It was hard to be d_____, but I felt that something was wrong with the whole b_____.
2. 'I'm a b_____man,' he said. 'I'm d_____ly not in b_____ to give money away.'
3. Although the two look s_____r, they are really quite s_____e things.
4. There was a strong s_____ity between the twins, even though they'd been brought up s_____ly.

Okay, let's get down to b_____s. First we s_____e the picture from the frame, then you put back the fake. They're so s_____r no one will notice — d_____ly no one. We leave the gallery s_____ly, you by the b_____men's entrance: I leave by the back door. We stay s_____e until we're d_____ly safe, but go to Nobby's by s_____r routes. Then we phone the owner and tell him about this strange s_____ity with the painting we've got. 'Bring the money in two s_____ cases,' we tell him, 'and your s_____ion from your painting will be over.' Then we're in b_____s: d_____ly in b_____s!

——25——

DIFFICULT WORDS 2

February is an awkward word. It just doesn't sound at all as if it's spelt like that. It's a miserable word which sounds shrivelled up — rather like the month itself, really, cold and dismal.

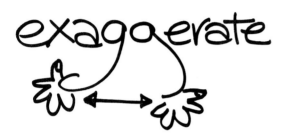

Exaggerate is a strange one: it's the two gs that cause the problem. They sound all right, but it always looks as if there's one too many. Try remembering the one that got away.

Environment is easy to mis-spell, too. Here it's the n in the middle that often gets left out. It means a place or setting — a working environment or a home environment, for example. It's also used to mean the nature world, when people talk of conserving the environment.

Now try these!

1. In F_____, new figures were published by the Department of the E_____.
2. E_____al Health Officers will examine the hotel in F_____.
3. It was not easy to e_____ the importance of the book.
4. He spoke quietly and without e_____ation.

Fellow e_____alists, welcome to the F_____y meeting. I can't e_____ the importance of preserving the e_____ in winter. To say that F_____ is the cruellest month is no e_____ion. E_____ally speaking, F_____ is the low point of the year. E_____ed claims have been made that e_____alists are cranks. Untrue! I'm delighted to launch our new campaign for e_____al protection: 'Save a worm this F_____!'

—— DIFFICULT WORDS 3 ——

Some words are spelt with an x or an s which is followed by a c. Others, though, have an x or an s which isn't followed by a c. So it can be tricky to sort out which spelling is right for a particular word, especially since there's no easy rule to follow.

Excellent, for example, does have a c after the x. If you excel at something, or anything you do is excellent, it's so good that it stands out above everything else. So try remembering the spelling like the drawing, with the c in a class of its own.

Exercise, though, doesn't have a c after the x. This is true whether you're talking about physical exercises or the ones on this page. Whether it's an aerobic work-out or a maths problem, exercise is spelt the same — without a c after the x.

Words with s and c are difficult ones, too.

There's **fascinate,** which has both letters. It's the same for other forms of the word, too — fascinating, fascinated and fascination all have the same spelling.

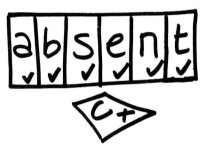

On the other hand, **absent** has no c. Other forms of the word follow the same spelling — absence, absentee and absenteeism; not a c in sight.

Now try these!

1. It was an e_____ idea to e_____ the dog before breakfast.
2. She kept in e_____ shape by taking regular e_____.
3. There was a f_____ing reason for his a_____ce that morning.
4. F_____ion with breakfast television has caused much a_____eeism.

Losing money through a_____ce from work? Has life lost its f_____ion! You need Ron Arkwright's e_____e album. Get in shape to the f_____ing sounds of Bert Twinge, with an e_____t commentary by megastar Ron himself, as used in e_____e periods throughout Wormwood Scrubs. You'll e_____l: your friends will be f_____ted. No more a_____eeism from work: your body will be in e_____t shape. Everybody's e_____sing with good old Ron — heavy breathing was never so f_____ing.

— DIFFICULT WORDS 4 —

Here are some words which often go wrong.

First of all, **strength.** Often the t gets left out, or another h somehow gets into the word, or it's spelt strongth. But it's just strength — the stuff that weightlifters have a lot of.

Maintenance is another one. It's the e in the middle that confuses you. It comes from maintain — so why does it change to maintenance? Whatever the reason, the e is there, and it's maintenance. Try thinking of it as what you do to cars on ramps, as shown in the picture.

Words which are related to numbers are awkward too. **Fourth** should be simple enough — it's only four with th stuck on the end. Somehow, though, the u tends to get lost. Think of it as 4th with our in the middle.

Eighth is another odd one. It's only eight with an extra h, but it still looks odd — can you think of another English word which ends in hth? Try thinking of it as part of a bar of chocolate, like the one in the drawing.

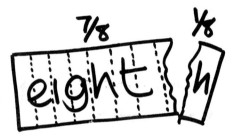

Now try these!

1. M_____ of staff levels at their present s_____ is not possible.
2. People of average s_____ are quite capable of routine car m_____.
3. An e_____ of an inch is called an e_____, but a f_____ is called a quarter.
4. The twenty-e_____ annual works outing will be held on the f_____ of May.

The e_____ item on your agenda, brothers, is the f_____ annual 'M_____ is S_____'

campaign. We know that motor m_____ makes sense, but does anyone else? An e_____ of cars have no proper m_____ and only a twenty-f_____ are serviced by recognised dealers. No wonder there's no s_____ in their pistons. An e_____ is not enough, brothers. Go out and get in more cars. By the f_____ of next month, I want m_____ contracts for at least another e_____ of these motors. For the f_____ time, brothers, I tell you — 'M_____ is S_____!'